• IN THIS PICTURE •

Can you find all the hidden objects?

CREATED BY ELLE SIMMS

ISBN-13: 978-1979061575

For Mylah Rose

In this book there are many objects to discover.
Some will be easy to spot. Ohers may be more difficult.

Some objects will be out in the open, like this.

And some may be partially hidden.

Some objects may look different than you expected. For example, mouse could mean...

This.   Or this.   Or this.   Or this.

BASKET CASE

In this picture you will find...

- [ ] 2 bears
- [ ] 2 butterflies
- [ ] 2 frogs
- [ ] 2 glass marbles
- [ ] 2 rubber ducks
- [ ] 4 leaf clover
- [ ] autumn leaf
- [ ] bunch of carrots
- [ ] ball of white string
- [ ] ball of yarn
- [ ] bird (starling)
- [ ] books
- [ ] cat
- [ ] chipmunk
- [ ] Christmas ornaments
- [ ] coffee beans
- [ ] coin
- [ ] compass
- [ ] crown
- [ ] dolphin
- [ ] dragonfly
- [ ] electrical plug
- [ ] elephant
- [ ] evergreen tree
- [ ] paper money
- [ ] fountain pen
- [ ] gold ring
- [ ] guitar
- [ ] hammer
- [ ] ice cream cone
- [ ] keyboard
- [ ] ladybug
- [ ] letter H
- [ ] necklace
- [ ] orange flower
- [ ] owl
- [ ] parrot
- [ ] phone booth
- [ ] piggy bank
- [ ] pterodactyl
- [ ] pumpkin
- [ ] purple flower
- [ ] rabbit
- [ ] raspberry
- [ ] satellite
- [ ] SD memory card
- [ ] shield
- [ ] speaker
- [ ] spiderweb
- [ ] starfish
- [ ] tiara
- [ ] tin bird
- [ ] tractor
- [ ] trumpet
- [ ] watch
- [ ] wooden duck
- [ ] wooden spoon
- [ ] yellow flower

ABANDONED

In this picture you will find...

- baby bottle
- BBQ grill
- beetle
- biohazard symbol
- bonsai tree
- book
- broom
- cardboard box
- cat
- chest
- child on a rocking horse
- chipmunk
- coffee cart
- dog
- drum
- Egyptian sculpture
- fish

- gear
- guinea pig
- handprint
- LOVE
- mail drop box
- medieval house
- motorcycle
- newspapers
- old black and white photo
- old transistor radio
- pegasus
- pig
- pigeon
- rabbit
- reclining figure
- rhinoceros
- screwdriver

- skeleton
- smile
- snail
- snake
- stack of stones
- street lamp
- tombstone
- toy spaceship
- travelling teddy bear
- umbrella
- vase of flowers
- violin
- vulture
- watch
- windmill
- wooden crate

WHAT-THE-SAURUS?

In this picture you will find...

- 5 bottles
- 6 birds
- 11 dinosaurs
- airplane
- antlers
- apple
- arched window
- bird house
- boat
- books
- butterfly
- cat
- clock

- cupcake
- cutting board with food
- dinosaur bones
- dish sponges
- DVD
- fabric hen
- fish
- giraffe
- gold picture frame
- hat
- iguana
- jug
- lightbulb

- pocket knife
- pretzel
- slice of pie
- squash
- sushi rolls
- teapot
- teddy bear
- tennis ball
- toilet paper roll
- trumpet
- umbrella
- watch
- watering can

NOT WHAT IT'S CHALKED UP TO BE

In this picture you will find...

- ☐ 2 birds
- ☐ 2 pigs
- ☐ 2 toy giraffes
- ☐ 3 autumn leaves
- ☐ airplane
- ☐ bandage
- ☐ baseball
- ☐ books
- ☐ car key
- ☐ cat
- ☐ cherry
- ☐ chess piece
- ☐ chicken drumstick
- ☐ city skyline
- ☐ crab
- ☐ dog
- ☐ dolphin
- ☐ dragon
- ☐ fairy

- ☐ fan
- ☐ fish bones
- ☐ flute
- ☐ four leaf clover
- ☐ hat
- ☐ hen
- ☐ hippo
- ☐ housefly
- ☐ kangaroo
- ☐ kerosene lamp
- ☐ knight in armor
- ☐ maybe
- ☐ MOM
- ☐ mosquito
- ☐ moth
- ☐ mouse
- ☐ person riding a bike
- ☐ poseable wooden body
- ☐ rain boots

- ☐ seahorse
- ☐ ship
- ☐ stagecoach
- ☐ star
- ☐ stethoscope
- ☐ tiger
- ☐ tin box
- ☐ tree
- ☐ tropical island
- ☐ turtle
- ☐ two pocket knives
- ☐ umbrella
- ☐ unicorn
- ☐ wagon wheel
- ☐ wings
- ☐ wooden heart frame
- ☐ yellow flower

MOON LANDING PHOTOBOMBERS

In this picture you will find...

- ☐ 1 ghost
- ☐ 2 cardboard boxes
- ☐ 2 satellites
- ☐ 3 UFOs
- ☐ 14 space creatures
- ☐ bones
- ☐ bucket
- ☐ candy cane
- ☐ cauliflower
- ☐ DVD
- ☐ Earth
- ☐ flower

- ☐ happy squash
- ☐ ice cream cone
- ☐ lizard on a flying carpet
- ☐ mushrooms
- ☐ old fashioned toilet
- ☐ poop emoji
- ☐ railroad sign
- ☐ stack of rocks
- ☐ clock
- ☐ coral
- ☐ dollar sign
- ☐ doughnut

- ☐ eggs
- ☐ elephant
- ☐ hamburger
- ☐ house
- ☐ ladder
- ☐ money
- ☐ polar bear
- ☐ Saturn
- ☐ teddy bear
- ☐ toilet paper
- ☐ tree
- ☐ young plant

CHILL AND GRILL

In this picture you will find...

- ☐ 2 anchors
- ☐ 2 coconuts
- ☐ 2 monkeys
- ☐ 2 pineapples
- ☐ 3 parrots
- ☐ 3 starfish
- ☐ 4 boats
- ☐ 5 seashells
- ☐ 6 fish

- ☐ banana (bunch)
- ☐ banana (single)
- ☐ beach sandal
- ☐ bottle
- ☐ cocktail umbrella
- ☐ coral
- ☐ crab
- ☐ diver
- ☐ dog

- ☐ fishing nets
- ☐ license plate
- ☐ lizard
- ☐ pelican
- ☐ pirate flag
- ☐ seahorse
- ☐ stack of rocks
- ☐ whale

FANTASTICAL

In this picture you will find...

- [ ] 2 fairies
- [ ] 14 butterflies
- [ ] beach chair
- [ ] campfire
- [ ] castle
- [ ] coat of arms
- [ ] crocodile
- [ ] crystal ball
- [ ] dragon
- [ ] elf girl
- [ ] floating island

- [ ] girl with unicorn
- [ ] hanging basket of flowers
- [ ] jug
- [ ] lantern
- [ ] mechanical snail
- [ ] outhouse
- [ ] plumbing pipes
- [ ] polar bear
- [ ] potato chips
- [ ] pot of flowers
- [ ] rabbit

- [ ] rubber duck
- [ ] signpost
- [ ] statue with flute
- [ ] statue with jug
- [ ] sunflower patch
- [ ] toast
- [ ] umbrella
- [ ] watermelon slices
- [ ] whale
- [ ] window
- [ ] woman riding a horse

WINTER BLUES

In this picture you will find...

- [ ] 4 butterflies
- [ ] angel statue
- [ ] basket
- [ ] bird wearing a hat
- [ ] carousel horse
- [ ] cat
- [ ] chair
- [ ] clothesline
- [ ] compass
- [ ] cowboy boot
- [ ] crab
- [ ] crown
- [ ] deer
- [ ] dog
- [ ] dolphin
- [ ] Earth

- [ ] electric razor
- [ ] eyeball
- [ ] feather
- [ ] flag garland
- [ ] flower
- [ ] grater
- [ ] ice cream cone
- [ ] ice skate
- [ ] iron
- [ ] jellyfish
- [ ] jug
- [ ] key
- [ ] kite
- [ ] light bulb
- [ ] lighthouse
- [ ] lizard

- [ ] map of the world
- [ ] microphone
- [ ] milk can
- [ ] number 5
- [ ] panda
- [ ] rabbit
- [ ] rainbow
- [ ] rooster
- [ ] rubber duck in a tub
- [ ] seagull
- [ ] snowy owl
- [ ] stack of mugs
- [ ] tall bird
- [ ] woolly mammoth
- [ ] yeti

WRITING ON THE WALL

In this picture you will find...

- ☐ 2 horses
- ☐ 3 cats
- ☐ accordion
- ☐ bike
- ☐ block of cheese
- ☐ blueberries
- ☐ car
- ☐ cheeseburger
- ☐ chef
- ☐ clock
- ☐ deer
- ☐ dinosaur
- ☐ diver
- ☐ elephants in a row

- ☐ fire extinguisher
- ☐ fish
- ☐ flute
- ☐ fried egg
- ☐ garbage can
- ☐ glass bottle
- ☐ goldfish
- ☐ grand piano
- ☐ hamster
- ☐ kayak
- ☐ lipstick print
- ☐ mango
- ☐ monster
- ☐ moose

- ☐ motorcycle
- ☐ nesting doll
- ☐ newspaper
- ☐ pencil
- ☐ pirate
- ☐ pretzel
- ☐ raspberry
- ☐ rubber boots
- ☐ stop sign
- ☐ toy van
- ☐ tractor
- ☐ traffic cone

DESERT DREAM

In this picture you will find...

- [ ] 2 camels
- [ ] 2 pairs of sunglasses
- [ ] 4 horses
- [ ] 11 fish and 1 ray
- [ ] angel
- [ ] armadillo
- [ ] autumn leaf
- [ ] bean bag chair
- [ ] bed
- [ ] boat
- [ ] bones
- [ ] book
- [ ] boots
- [ ] bridge
- [ ] cactus

- [ ] calf
- [ ] carousel horse
- [ ] child
- [ ] crown of flowers
- [ ] giraffe
- [ ] hourglass
- [ ] kangaroo
- [ ] keyboard
- [ ] lemur
- [ ] lizard
- [ ] medieval banner
- [ ] metal tub
- [ ] mouse
- [ ] Noah's ark
- [ ] old car

- [ ] pail and shovel
- [ ] piñata
- [ ] planet
- [ ] puzzle piece
- [ ] pyramids
- [ ] sand sculpture
- [ ] scarf
- [ ] selfie stick
- [ ] statue (head)
- [ ] traffic cone
- [ ] turkey
- [ ] turtle
- [ ] umbrella
- [ ] winter tree

FOR THE BIRDS

In this picture you will find...

- ☐ 2 airplanes
- ☐ 2 cats
- ☐ 2 sheep
- ☐ 2 signs
- ☐ 2 snails
- ☐ 2 spiders
- ☐ autumn squash
- ☐ banana
- ☐ balloon animal
- ☐ bear
- ☐ bell
- ☐ Christmas tree
- ☐ clock
- ☐ cob of corn
- ☐ cocktail umbrella
- ☐ crab
- ☐ cup of coffee
- ☐ daisy
- ☐ dinosaur
- ☐ doll

- ☐ dolphin
- ☐ dragonfly
- ☐ fan
- ☐ flowery branch
- ☐ fly
- ☐ grater
- ☐ hand
- ☐ hot chocolate
- ☐ key
- ☐ knitting
- ☐ laurel wreath
- ☐ letter C
- ☐ mandarin duck
- ☐ monster
- ☐ moustache
- ☐ mushroom
- ☐ music note
- ☐ old wooden cart
- ☐ picture frame
- ☐ pinecone

- ☐ ping pong paddles
- ☐ poinsettia
- ☐ pomegranate
- ☐ rabbit
- ☐ red shoes
- ☐ rose
- ☐ screwdriver
- ☐ seagull
- ☐ snake
- ☐ squirrel
- ☐ stack of rocks
- ☐ statue
- ☐ sunflowers
- ☐ sunglasses
- ☐ swordfish
- ☐ train
- ☐ treasure chest
- ☐ tree stump
- ☐ window with shutters

WELCOME TO THE CIRCUS

In this picture you will find...

- ☐ 2 buckets of popcorn
- ☐ 3 clowns
- ☐ 6 airplanes
- ☐ apple (caramel covered)
- ☐ apple (plain)
- ☐ apple turnover
- ☐ APPROVED
- ☐ balloon animal
- ☐ baseball bat
- ☐ bigtop tent
- ☐ blue chest
- ☐ broccoli
- ☐ cabbage
- ☐ candy corn
- ☐ carousel
- ☐ child with butterfly
- ☐ Christmas ornament

- ☐ deer head
- ☐ door hinge
- ☐ elephant
- ☐ flowers (basket)
- ☐ flowers (bouquet)
- ☐ gold wings
- ☐ lantern
- ☐ leopard
- ☐ lizard
- ☐ marbles
- ☐ MAYBE
- ☐ money
- ☐ moustache
- ☐ orange basket
- ☐ painting
- ☐ penguin
- ☐ playing card

- ☐ policemen
- ☐ postage stamps
- ☐ recorder
- ☐ shoes
- ☐ slipper
- ☐ smartphone
- ☐ stack of books
- ☐ sunflower
- ☐ tambourine
- ☐ ticket
- ☐ top hat
- ☐ trapeze artist
- ☐ umbrella
- ☐ vintage typewriter
- ☐ violin
- ☐ X-ray

STEAMPUNKED

In this picture you will find...

- [ ] 2 birds
- [ ] 2 doors
- [ ] 3 dragons
- [ ] 3 headed monster
- [ ] 12 flying machines
- [ ] barbed wire
- [ ] barrel
- [ ] bed frame
- [ ] bell
- [ ] bike chain
- [ ] books
- [ ] cactus
- [ ] camera
- [ ] cat
- [ ] clock

- [ ] creature with long trunk
- [ ] EMERGENCY
- [ ] fan
- [ ] fancy brass coffee pot
- [ ] fire hydrant
- [ ] floating eyeballs
- [ ] fried eggs
- [ ] frog
- [ ] gears
- [ ] globe
- [ ] hammer
- [ ] heart
- [ ] high heeled shoe
- [ ] jewelry box
- [ ] key

- [ ] kiwifruit
- [ ] lamp
- [ ] leather bag
- [ ] lion head door knocker
- [ ] lipstick
- [ ] locked chest
- [ ] long stemmed rose
- [ ] old car
- [ ] orange
- [ ] signpost
- [ ] street lamp
- [ ] teapot
- [ ] toy train
- [ ] turtle

SANTA'S OFFICE

In this picture you will find...

- 3 dolls
- 5 Christmas cards
- 6 teddy bears
- 7 round ornaments
- alarm clock
- baby carriage
- baseball
- bell ornament
- bird
- candy cane
- chandelier
- child on a rocking horse
- Christmas tree
- clock
- cowboy hat
- crayons
- doughnut
- elf
- fidget spinner
- fish mobile
- gingerbread house
- gold feather
- HO HO HO!
- horseshoe
- hot chocolate
- joker
- leaf
- mailbox
- nativity scene
- North Pole sign
- owl
- paper airplane
- poinsettia
- puzzle cube
- puzzle piece
- reindeer
- robot
- rubber duck
- sack of gifts
- Santa
- Santa toy
- snowman
- spinning top
- squirrel
- tomato
- toy car
- wagon
- zebra

HOME SWEET HOME

In this picture you will find...

- [ ] 2 birds on a branch
- [ ] 2 ladybugs
- [ ] 2 tiny houses
- [ ] 2 trucks
- [ ] 3 Easter eggs
- [ ] aardvark
- [ ] APPROVED
- [ ] astronaut
- [ ] bird cage
- [ ] broccoli
- [ ] bunch of carrots
- [ ] can of pencils
- [ ] cat
- [ ] check yes or no
- [ ] clock
- [ ] coffee beans
- [ ] dog in his bed

- [ ] duck crossing sign
- [ ] fan
- [ ] fire hydrant
- [ ] framed photo
- [ ] frogs on toadstools
- [ ] garden gnome
- [ ] garlic bulb
- [ ] goose
- [ ] heart shaped frame
- [ ] helicopter
- [ ] horseshoe
- [ ] kiwifruit
- [ ] leather bag
- [ ] loaf of bread
- [ ] money
- [ ] monster
- [ ] old boots

- [ ] owl
- [ ] pinwheel
- [ ] pocket watch
- [ ] potatoes
- [ ] purple flowers
- [ ] soccer ball
- [ ] snake
- [ ] space shuttle
- [ ] sun
- [ ] surprised potato
- [ ] teacup
- [ ] thermometer
- [ ] turkey
- [ ] unicycle
- [ ] water spigot
- [ ] wind chimes
- [ ] wreath

THERE WAS AN OLD WOMAN...

In this picture you will find...

- [ ] 2 birds on a branch
- [ ] 2 butterflies
- [ ] 2 fairies
- [ ] 2 frogs
- [ ] 2 guinea pigs
- [ ] 2 hats
- [ ] 2 paintings
- [ ] 2 starfish
- [ ] 4 snails
- [ ] artist's easel
- [ ] artist's palette
- [ ] balloons
- [ ] beach chair
- [ ] beetle
- [ ] Believe
- [ ] bell
- [ ] bench
- [ ] bowtie
- [ ] broken egg
- [ ] broom
- [ ] cherry

- [ ] chocolate rabbit
- [ ] clock
- [ ] clover
- [ ] daisy
- [ ] dragonfly
- [ ] duck crossing sign
- [ ] empty flower pot
- [ ] fish
- [ ] flag garland
- [ ] flower crown
- [ ] glass bottle
- [ ] glowing eyes
- [ ] gold ring
- [ ] hanging flowers
- [ ] heart
- [ ] hedgehog(ish) creature
- [ ] key
- [ ] kite
- [ ] kiwifruit
- [ ] ladybug
- [ ] lantern

- [ ] LAUGH
- [ ] lizard
- [ ] mailbox
- [ ] mermaid sign
- [ ] mouse
- [ ] moustache
- [ ] old books
- [ ] pencil
- [ ] puzzle piece
- [ ] recorder
- [ ] rubber duck
- [ ] seahorse
- [ ] squirrel
- [ ] striped bag
- [ ] teddy bear
- [ ] umbrella
- [ ] unicycle
- [ ] wind chime
- [ ] wind sock
- [ ] wings
- [ ] wooden spoon

MONSTER-OUS!

Can you spot the monster hiding in the rice fields?

CAN YOU SPIN IT?

Your mission is to find the lost fidget spinner.

BOOKWORM

Where is this worm?

DID YOU LIKE THIS BOOK?

Please leave a review.

www.amazon.com/author/ellesimms

ENJOY PUZZLES?

For hours of fun, check out these titles.

AVAILABLE NOW

Watch for more books by Elle Simms scheduled for release in 2018.

Made in the USA
Coppell, TX
24 July 2020